# LEADER DEVELOPMENT, LEARNING AGILITY, AND THE ARMY PROFESSION

## COL Brian J. Reed[1]

## Abstract

The current Army Profession campaign makes the case for a re-evaluation and assessment of the Army as a profession and the attributes of the Army Professional. Leadership entails the repetitive exercise of discretionary judgments, all highly moral in nature, and represents the core function of the Army Professional's military art. Leader development is an investment required to maintain the Army as a profession. The profession is maintained by leaders who place a high priority on leader development and invest themselves and the resources of the profession to develop professionals and future leaders at all levels. This project outlines a model for leader development anchored in learning agility and the notion that learning agile leaders apply previous learning and embrace learning in new, novel, or ill-defined environments. Learning agile leaders are adaptable. These leaders see actions that are different from the norm and readjust in an appropriate manner. If mission command is the operating principle for the Army and given the context of today's operational environment, then adaptable leaders are an absolute necessity. Leader development systems must enhance and maximize one's motivation and ability to develop, and the overall Army culture must be supportive of such a process.

---

[1] COL Brian Reed is a Senior Service College Fellow at Teacher's College, Columbia University and the Center for the Army Profession and Ethic. He graduated in 1989 from the U.S. Military Academy and was commissioned as an infantry officer. COL Reed has served in a variety of command and staff positions. Most recently, he was the Battalion Commander of 1st Battalion 24th Infantry (Stryker). COL Reed has a Ph.D. in Sociology from the University of Maryland. He can be contacted at brian.reed@us.army.mil.

*A day after being sworn in as the new Army Chief of Staff, General Raymond T. Odierno laid out some priorities for his tenure...Future leaders must be adaptable, agile, and able to operate in a threat environment that includes a combination of regular warfare, irregular warfare, terrorist activity, and criminality.* [1]

*Soldiers must...be trained, equipped and trusted to operate autonomously...Such leaders must be able to recognize change and then lead others through that change. They must empower subordinates and create an environment where leaders are allowed to grow.* [2]

## Introduction

For the military, operational environments are a composite of the conditions, circumstances, and influences that affect capabilities and decisions and include all enemy, friendly, and neutral systems as well as the physical environment, governance, local resources, culture, and technology. [3] Such environments require leaders who are adaptive and agile and are able to make ethical, informed decisions efficiently and effectively. Current Army doctrine calls for "mission command," "task and purpose," and "intent based" orders to guide the execution of military operations. The premise behind such concepts is that we expect trained and resourced leaders to operate within broadly defined boundaries, and armed with the commander's intent, to successfully accomplish a large variety of missions. The Army's emphasis is on decentralized execution based on mission orders. Appropriately, the focus is on the purpose of the operation rather than on the details of how to perform the assigned task. [4] This calls for ethical, adaptable leaders.

Anecdotally, many Army leaders would agree with the preceding paragraph. Those who have spent time in either Afghanistan or Iraq, and have worked within an enormous area of operations, understand that subordinate leaders need to be resourced and entrusted to make decisions and operate many, many miles from the unit's higher command. This demands decentralized execution based on mission orders. Such a concept is not new. This is similar to how units (Allied and German) conducted operations in World War II. The scale of the battlefield and the limitations in communication technology made this a necessity. Combat operations in Korea were conducted along the same lines. Arguably, it is with the war in Vietnam where there is shift in how commanders exerted command and control. The advent of the helicopter and technological advances in communications gave commanders the ability to garner close to "real time" situational awareness and thereby exert greater, centralized control of subordinate units.

After Vietnam, the Army's focus was on Cold War operations with a relatively predictable enemy. The expected nature of the European battlefield – one large campaign with multiple units involved side by side along a broad front – made it essential to centralize and efficiently manage various elements of combat power.[5] Subordinate units collected information to support senior commanders' decisions; rarely did the reverse occur. Most assets and most of the capability to analyze the information they gathered resided at division headquarters and higher. Similar arrangements governed the operational planning and employment of artillery, aviation, transportation, and a host of other assets. A centralized battlefield required a centralized Army.[6]

Unlike the relatively stable and predictable environment of the late Cold War, today's battlefields evolve rapidly. They differ greatly from place to place and from one time to another. The luxury of being able to predict problems that units will face is gone, and so is the ability to work out best solutions in advance.[7] As an example, a brigade commander in the post-9/11 operational environment has an enormous and complex fighting organization, complete with multiple and competing tasks. Units are spread over hundreds of miles. Company operations run from combat outposts and must be nested with the brigade commander's intent (2 command levels up). Clearly, the brigade commander cannot be physically present everywhere to ensure that company commanders are operating within that intent. Present day communication platforms allow higher commanders to access close to real time information on friendly force disposition, and the increasing number of requirements for pre-mission approval and post-mission de-briefings add to the commander's situational awareness. In reality, however, given the dispersion of forces and the constraints of terrain, weather, and other battlefield factors, the brigade commander must trust subordinate leaders to conduct operations within the stated intent and to exercise decentralized decision making within the complexity of the operational environment. This is mission command.

Mission command demands that when necessary, unit leadership should coordinate and act together even without receiving specific direction from above. The result will be an evolving leadership style that requires leaders and commanders to focus their attention downward and outward onto the battlefield.[8] The adaptation of mission command increases demands for responsibility and innovation at all levels. These demands place a greater premium on (1) adaptability to emergent situations, (2) operating with and within joint, interagency and multinational organizations, (3) rapid responsiveness and (4) the mental and physical agility to capitalize on opportunities in the field.[9] Key to the Army's adjustment is the ability to support leader development and empowering adaptability in individuals for operations in the current and future complex environment.

Leaders do not automatically "learn" about mission command. It is not something that simply happens to them, either at the higher or lower levels of unit command. It needs to be how we do business all of the time. During home station operations, mission orders and decentralized execution should be the modus operandi. If the Army is going to trust junior leaders to make critical decisions on an isolated outpost, they must be trusted to make similar decisions during training and normal, routine operations at home station.

Equally important is how such a mission command approach is engrained in institutional leader development systems. Mission command is not a concept solely within the purview of the operational force. Such an approach needs to be part of the very fabric of the Army organization and is taught and highlighted in Army education and training and reinforced in the personnel assignment process. Specific broadening assignments that allow for personal, educational, and developmental opportunities will result in more effective leaders in this increasingly complex operational environment. Traditionally, the Army culture values and rewards those junior leaders who have extensive amounts of time in the tactical arena. Such positions are key to the development of effective tactical commanders. In this changing world, however, education and broadening experiences are instrumental to developing imaginative operational and strategic leaders, those who will master the current and emerging domestic and global complexities.[10]

The Profession and Adaptable Leaders

When thinking of professions, the coins of the realm are often considered to be expertise and the knowledge underlying it.[11] More so than other occupations,

5

professions focus on generating expert knowledge and the ability of its members to apply that expertise to new situations. Medical professionals perfect medical techniques to apply to patients, attorneys apply legal expertise in courtrooms, and the military develops new technologies, capabilities, and strategies to provide for the common defense.[12] Such professional expertise is ultimately validated by the client and forms the basis for the trust between the profession and the society served. Furthermore, the success in the professional application of expertise results from effective and ethical application.[13]

To call an occupation a profession is usually to make a positive normative judgment about the work being done – work required for the well being of society.[14] Such work is compared to particular standards that prescribe how professional activities ought to be done if they are good. For the Army Profession, three prescriptive factors mark the normative expectations of the profession: *expertise* which occurs through a system of professional development, education, and training; *jurisdiction* within which expert knowledge is applied; and *legitimacy* which is a result of the unquestioned trust between the Army Profession and the society it serves.[15] Because of its responsibility for wielding deadly force to defend the nation and the Constitution, the Army Profession had developed throughout the course of its history an ethic that provided the objective norms and standards for the behavior of the profession and its members. Influenced by American society and the Army Professionals themselves, the ethic required that members transcend the norms of the pack, particularly when under chaotic and stressful situations, such as those that exist in combat.[16]

Fifteen years ago, references to counter-insurgency in Afghanistan and Iraq, modular brigades, mission command, combat outposts, and the like would have been virtually meaningless to many, if not all, in the Army.[17] Today, these references are recognizable to most and represent just a handful of the important influences on the Army over the past several years. In the face of the evolving nature of the battlefield, repeated deployments, and force structure and budget decisions, the Army has demonstrated great strengths in some areas, yet struggles in others. With this as the backdrop, the Army leadership directed a review of the Army profession and determined that it is "essential that we take a hard look at ourselves to ensure we understand what we have been through over the past nine years, how we have changed, and how we must adapt to succeed in an era of persistent conflict."[18]

Within this context, the current Army Profession (AP) Campaign has identified a hallmark of the Army Professional[19] to be the "repetitive exercise of discretionary judgments, all highly moral in nature…[T]his represents the core function of the Army professional's military art, whether leading a patrol in combat or making a major policy or budget decision in the Pentagon."[20] Furthermore, it is the Professional Ethic that governs the culture, and thus the actions, of the professional. The Ethic is the means of motivation and self control and derives its substance from primarily three sources: (1) functional imperatives of the profession; (2) national values, beliefs, and norms; and (3) international laws and treaties.[21] While the Professional Ethic treats mission accomplishment as a moral imperative, it also recognizes the moral and legal limitations that shape our judgment regarding the application of military force.[22]

The Army Professional demonstrates leadership in volatile, uncertain, complex, and ambiguous situations within a framework of standards for conduct and performance. Starting with the premise that the Army is a profession then the individuals in that profession are experts. The Army Professional possesses expert knowledge that is manifested as unique skills of the individual and by larger units. The repetitive exercise of discretionary judgments is one of those skills.

The expertise to make discretionary judgments is rooted in the professional's ability to be adaptable as a leader. As General Odierno discussed in the opening vignette, Army leaders must be adaptable. This adaptability is a component of the expert skill set of the Army Professional. Adaptability entails "cognitive and behavioral capabilities with regard to (1) maintaining situational awareness and recognizing when behavioral changes are needed…(2) changing behavior in a way that produces more effective organizational functioning; and (3) evaluating the outcome and making further adjustments, as needed, to achieve the desired results."[23] To be adaptable requires leaders to make an effective change in response to an altered situation. It is the ability of leaders to see actions that are different from the norm and to readjust in an appropriate manner. The implications of adaptive leadership for individual leaders entail a shift from centralized top-down authority, which emphasizes control and directed actions, to a process more about creativity, adaptation, indirect and multidirectional control,[24] or, within the framework of today's operational environments, decentralized execution, mission command, and intent based orders.

Leadership can be thought of as social process that reflects the interactive nature of social network dynamics that occur among people in an organizational context.[25]

Such a context is influenced by factors that complicate the operational environment in which the professional exists. Furthermore, leadership includes attention to common goals. Leaders and followers have a mutual purpose. Attention to common goals gives leadership an ethical underpinning because it stresses the need for leaders to work with followers to achieve selected goals.[26] Stressing mutuality lessens the possibility that leaders might act toward followers in ways that are forced or unethical.[27]

Leadership does not happen automatically and certainly one's ability to exercise discretionary judgments adaptively is not necessarily a routine action. In this regard, leadership, or more precisely leading, as a micro-level phenomenon, is a process of individual influence that reflects the cognitive and behavioral complexity of individual leaders.[28] More to the point, this process of leadership with its "cognitive and behavioral complexity" can be learned.

Creating, developing, and maintaining this expert knowledge, and embedding that knowledge in members of the profession is critical. This expertise includes how to maximize the effectiveness of the Army's people. It also includes professional development and engagement in academic fields relevant to Army training and education.[29] The Army's jurisdiction in which to exercise this expertise is ultimately legitimized by the demands of society as voiced by its civilian leaders.[30] Leadership, as one category of the Army Professional's expert knowledge, is applied in a jurisdiction ultimately defined by society, but negotiated between Army and civilian leaders.

Learning Agility

Since the Army Professional is now required to be far more adaptable to changing conditions than ever before, finding ways and means to support this newer and more demanding necessity is paramount.  One such support is the comparatively new construct in organizational and leadership research called learning agility – that is, the ability to apply previous learning and/or embrace learning in new, novel, or ill-defined environments.[31]

The expertise – or unique skill – of the Army Professional to ethically exercise discretionary judgments can be learned through learning agility.  Adaptability is an action and is, therefore, an outcome of learning agility.[32] Individuals and/or organizations cannot be adaptive without the capacity for continuous learning.[33]  A person learns from experiences that force him/her to step up and lead, preferably requiring one to stretch his/her capabilities and move beyond experiences to be effective.  Such experiences can be understood as crucible or trigger events – that is, transformative events that generate a learning point resulting in a script for further action in like circumstances.  A range of such events can occur at any time in one's life course.  If interpreted and processed, such trigger events will stimulate further leader development, as well as produce perhaps a new way of approaching a particular leadership issue, opportunity, challenge, or problem.[34]

Learning agility is enhanced by three types of behaviors: (1) seeking – seeking out new learning opportunities and ways of doing things, particularly in areas where success is uncertain; (2) performing – being able to manage oneself in challenging situations and dealing with new situations in a way that maximizes performance; and (3) reflecting – thinking about experiences to surface critical information.  However, there are also potential behavioral de-railers that may have an impact on one's ability to do the above: (1) risk aversion – prevents an individual from seeking out new opportunities that may guarantee success, but will ultimately inhibit learning; and (2) defensiveness – prevents an individual's ability to manage effectively new situations or bias the way one thinks about past experiences.[35]

For learning agility to be effective, the conditions within the organizational culture should exist that will foster such learning (enhance, not derail). In other words, the individual behaviors described in the preceding paragraph must also be manifested in the organization's culture. Organizational cultures are created by leaders, and one of the most decisive functions of leadership may well be the creation and the management of this culture. Considering Edgar Schein's seminal work on organizational culture, the term "culture" is reserved for the deeper level of basic assumptions and beliefs that are shared by members of an organization, that operate unconsciously, and that define in a basic "taken-for-granted" fashion an organization's view of itself and its environment. These assumptions and beliefs are learned responses to a group's problems of survival in its external environment and its problems of internal integration. They come to be taken for granted because they solve those problems repeatedly and reliably. This deeper level of assumptions is to be distinguished from the "artifacts" and "values" that are manifestations or surface levels of the culture, but not the essence of the culture.[36] Therefore, it is not satisfactory for leaders to simply state that the organization supports those behaviors that foster learning agility and discourage those that derail learning agility. Such espoused beliefs are superficial unless they are grounded in the underlying assumptions of the organization.

## Leader Developmental Readiness

The developmental readiness of an individual is an important pre-condition for learning agility to effectively result in an adaptive leader's ethical application of discretionary judgments. Leader developmental readiness is a combination of one's motivation and ability. A leader's motivation to develop "is promoted through interest and goals, learning goal orientation, and developmental efficacy", while a leader's ability to develop "is promoted through self awareness, self complexity, and meta-cognitive ability."[37] Leaders with higher levels of developmental readiness will be better able to reflect upon and make meaning out of events, challenges, and/or opportunities that can stimulate and accelerate positive leader development,[38] thus resulting in a more powerful experience during the learning agility process.[39]

Of the individual differences promoting motivation to develop,[40] research suggests that to engage intently in learning opportunities intrinsic motivation is necessary, which in turn requires tapping into one's interests and goals. Furthermore, an individual with a high learning goal orientation will see challenges as a way to improve and develop and will be more accepting of failure in the pursuit of self development. Finally, the third motivational component, developmental efficacy, represents a leader's level of confidence that he or she can develop and successfully employ the knowledge, skills, and abilities that are required in certain leadership contexts.

The first component promoting an individual's ability to develop,[41] self-awareness, is characterized by one's ability to reflect and use patterns of thinking and emotion in an open, positive, and learning oriented manner, which facilitates new learning. In turn, self complexity represents how a leader differentiates as well as integrates various sources and types of information. More complex leaders have more cognitive capacity with which to process, interpret, and appropriate new developmental experiences. The last ability component, meta-cognitive ability, facilitates "second order" thinking, and allows for a much deeper examination (beyond reflection) of one's own theory of leadership and to consider and make amendments to the theory on the basis of new experiences.

For the individual to be developmentally ready, the setting and context for positive leader development to occur and flourish must be established in the organizational culture. This culture must be supportive of leader development systems that promote developmental readiness. Enhancing leaders' levels of developmental readiness in the organization will prepare them to develop more fully from both planned developmental events and unplanned fortuitous events[42] (the very type of events linked to learning agility). Furthermore, as the individual leader's readiness increases, so too does the organization's culture for development. Leaders influence the leader development systems that their followers experience in organizations. Thus, to the extent that the leader is positive about and personally models development, it is more likely that he/she will promote positive development in others.[43]

A Model for Development

The figure below represents the theoretical construct outlined above. In short, high leader developmental readiness is comprised of one's increased motivation and ability to develop. This promotes learning agile leaders – that is, leaders with an increased ability to apply previous learning and/or embrace learning in new, novel, or ill defined environments, and who seek, perform, reflect, and are not risk averse or defensive. The organizational culture moderates the link between developmental readiness and learning agility and whether this succeeds or fails. Finally, learning agility results in adaptable leaders.

In order to be effective, Army leader development systems must capitalize on one's motivation and ability to develop as a leader. This cannot be isolated to platoons, companies, battalions, etc., but instead must be manifested throughout the depth and breadth of the Army Profession. Motivated and armed with the ability to develop as leaders, we can now grow learning agile leaders. Such leaders are adaptable and able to exercise discretionary judgments ethically in a volatile, uncertain, complex, and ambiguous operational environment, within the framework of the higher command's intent. This is the hallmark of the Army Professional.

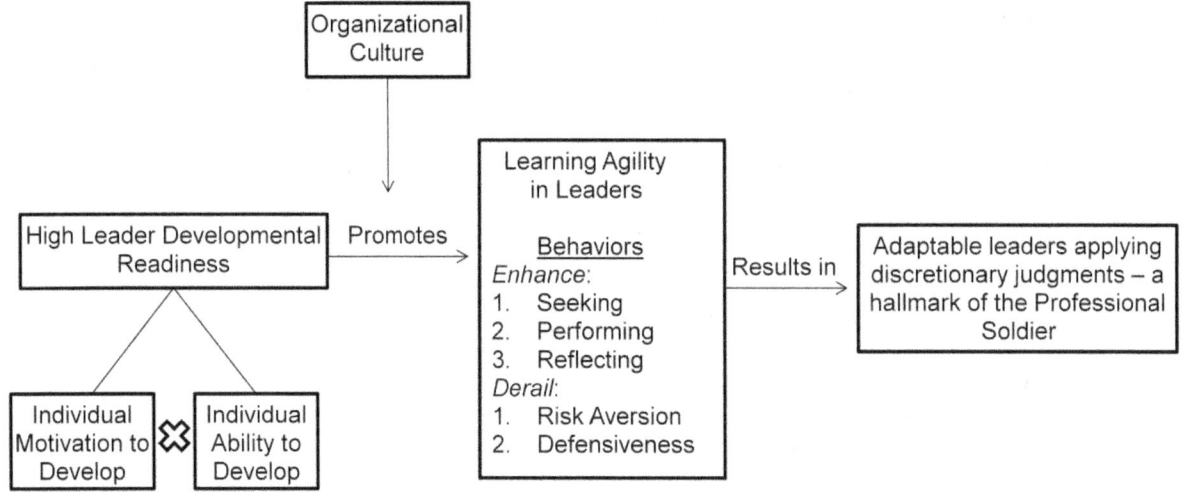

Research Question and Methods

This research project addresses the question: <u>are Army senior leaders above average with respect to learning agility</u>? The sample includes LTC/O5-level leaders and above, and Department of the Army (DA) civilian equivalents. Snowball sampling to collect the survey data resulted in a sample size of 89 respondents. These respondents accessed the survey on-line. The survey included several demographic questions and replicated the Burke (2010) working group research as closely as possible. A learning agility assessment survey was used which has been demonstrated to be reliable – consistent internally over time. Composed of 29 items the results of this survey produced scores on the two primary components of learning agility: learning enhancers (seeking, performing, reflecting) and learning de-railers (risk aversion, defensiveness).

In addition to addressing the primary research question, three other related questions were considered: (1) do senior leaders have high leader developmental readiness; (2) are senior leaders adaptable; and (3) is the Army's organizational culture supportive of learning agility? Hannah's (2010) measure of developmental readiness was used to assess the first question.[44] This measure consisted of seven survey items for each sub-component of leader developmental readiness. The self assessment adaptability measure from Pulakos et al (2002) was used for the second question.[45] This measure consisted of eight survey items. Like the learning agility survey questions, the results are self assessments and reflect what respondents believe about themselves. Finally, for the third question, the qualitative responses from the Army Profession survey were analyzed, specifically considering the questions pertaining to culture and leader development. The Center for the Army Profession and Ethic (CAPE) conducted this research as part of the on-going campaign on the Army Profession.

## Results and Analysis

*Sample Composition*

The sample consists of 89 respondents, of which 80.9% are male and 19.1% are female. The majority (75.3%) identify their race as White with 12.4% identifying themselves as Black or African American. Colonels make up 72.4% of the respondents while 16.1% are DA Civilian equivalents. The remainder are Lieutenant Colonels and one Major. There are no General Officers in the sample. The average age of the respondents is 44 years, and 92% of them have a graduate degree. In terms of branch, 43.9% are combat arms, 15.9% are combat support, and 40.2% are combat service support. Finally, the majority of the sample have been deployed. When asked the number of months they have been deployed since 11 September 2001 in support of combat operations in Iraq or Afghanistan, 22.5% of the respondents were deployed for more than 24 months with 24.7% having been deployed between 12 and 23 months. 20.2% of the respondents have never deployed.

To assess the representativeness of the sample, I used the active Colonel population given that over 70% of the sample identified as a Colonel. There are 4471 Colonels on active duty.[46] This sample is over-represented by women, but the sample is fairly representative when compared to the percentages of men and women in the armed forces as a whole.[47] In terms of race, branch, and education, the sample is fairly representative. With respect to numbers deployed since 9/11, the sample is over-represented in the category of over 24 months, but fairly representative in the others. Overall then, the sample is generally representative of the population and will permit

16

one to draw some inferences from the findings.  The sample and population

comparisons are represented in Table 1.

| | SAMPLE | POPULATION |
|---|---|---|
| Size | 89 | 4471 |
| Gender[48] | | |
| Men | 81% | 89%/86% |
| Women | 19% | 11%/14% |
| Race | | |
| White | 75% | 82% |
| Black | 12% | 11% |
| Other Races | 13% | 7% |
| Branch | | |
| Combat Arms | 44% | 40% |
| Combat Support | 16% | 14% |
| Combat Service Support | 40% | 46% |
| Graduate Degree | 92%[49] | 100% |
| Deployed Since 9/11 | | |
| 0 Months | 20% | 21% |
| 12 to 24 Months | 25% | 29% |
| Over 24 Months | 23% | 18% |

Table 1: Sample and Population Comparison

*Learning Agility*

The learning enhancer dimensions represent those behaviors that demonstrate

an appetite for learning (seeking), an ability to manage new and challenging situations

(performing), and a willingness to reflect on experience in order to surface learning

(reflecting).  Table 2 shows the overall respondents' mean scores for each dimension.

Also presented is the range of scores.  The higher the mean, the greater the

respondents demonstrate that learning enhancer dimension.  From the results, it is clear

17

that the respondents demonstrate a high affinity for those behaviors that enhance learning agility. Seeking and performing are the two highest scores which reflect, respectively, a tendency for these respondents to seek out new learning opportunities and to deal with new situations in a way that maximizes performance. Reflecting is the lowest score. This indicates that the respondents are less likely, compared to the other dimensions, to think about experiences to surface critical information.

The power of reflection should not be understated and a low score could be a reason for concern. Reflective observation, or learning by reflecting, entails observing carefully before making judgments, viewing issues from different perspectives, and looking for the meaning of things.[50] One needs to connect the conceptual with the concrete experience in order to make learning meaningful. This is done through active reflection. The conceptual, or abstract, is what one reads and thinks. The concrete is what one sees, feels, or touches – the experience.

To truly make the reflection active is done in interaction with others and can be facilitated through a process of Description/Interpretation/Evaluation and Knowledge: Description – what do you observe; Interpretation – how do you judge what you see; Evaluation and Knowledge – what knowledge do you bring to your interpretation and evaluation, or what do you need to know about in order to better your interpretation and evaluation. Reflection is therefore systematic, rigorous, and disciplined. It is not simply "thinking" about an experience. Reflection as a meaning making process moves the learner from one experience to the next with deeper understanding of its relationships with and connections to other experiences and ideas. At the start, however, this requires an attitude on the part of the learner that values the personal and intellectual growth of oneself and others.[51]

| | SEEKING | PERFORMING | REFLECTING | LEARNING ENHANCERS TOTAL |
|---|---|---|---|---|
| **Range** | 5 – 25 | 6 – 30 | 7 – 35 | 18 – 90 |
| **Overall Mean Scores** | 19.22 | 23.19 | 25.58 | 67.99 |

Table 2: Learning Enhancer Scores

The de-railer dimensions represent behaviors that may impede learning, such as becoming defensive when faced with challenges or given feedback (defensiveness), or seeking only comfortable situations in which success is likely but new learning will be limited (risk aversion). Table 3 presents the results for these dimensions with the possible range of scores and the overall respondents' mean scores. In this case, the lower score is more desired as this would indicate the limited impact of those behaviors that impede learning agility. For the respondents, the scores indicate a higher propensity toward these de-railing behaviors. In this sample, we see a higher inclination toward defensiveness and those behaviors that prevent one's ability to manage effectively new situations or bias the way one thinks about past experiences. Likewise is the tendency to be risk averse and therefore not to seek new opportunities for learning at the risk of unassured success.

| | DEFENSIVENESS | RISK AVERSION | LEARNING DE-RAILERS TOTAL |
|---|---|---|---|
| **Range** | 4 – 20 | 7 – 35 | 11 – 55 |
| **Overall Mean Scores** | 14.45 | 21.07 | 35.52 |

Table 3: Learning De-Railer Scores

Also analyzed were the learning agility scores for enhancing and de-railing behaviors while controlling for several variables. Table 4 shows the results for the behaviors when controlling for branch, months deployed since 11 September 2001, and gender. Of note, when considering branch, combat arms respondents are less likely to display the behaviors that de-rail learning agility while combat service support respondents are more likely to exhibit the behaviors that support learning agility. When looking at months deployed, those respondents who have not deployed are less likely to exhibit de-railing behaviors (less defensive and less risk averse). In general, deployed respondents are more likely to display enhancing behaviors (more seeking, performing, and reflecting) than the respondents who had not deployed. Finally, women are more reflecting and more risk averse than men.

| | SEEKING | PERFORMING | REFLECTING | DEFENSIVENESS | RISK AVERSION |
|---|---|---|---|---|---|
| Range | 5 – 25 | 6 – 30 | 7 – 35 | 4 – 20 | 7 – 35 |
| What is your branch? | | | | | |
| Combat Arms | 18.33 | 22.70 | 25.07 | 14.37 | 20.62 |
| Combat Support | 18.03 | 22.50 | 25.50 | 15.56 | 21.08 |
| Combat Service Support | 20.21 | 23.47 | 25.65 | 14.75 | 21.70 |
| Since 11 September 2001, how many months have you spent deployed in support of combat operations in either Iraq or Afghanistan? | | | | | |
| 0 | 18.82 | 22.70 | 23.92 | 12.82 | 20.27 |
| less than 12 | 20.85 | 23.76 | 24.38 | 15.84 | 21.69 |
| 12 – 23 | 19.00 | 23.09 | 25.37 | 15.58 | 21.39 |
| 24 or more | 18.97 | 23.45 | 26.36 | 13.41 | 20.93 |
| Are you male or female? | | | | | |
| Female | 19.75 | 23.25 | 26.02 | 14.86 | 21.91 |
| Male | 19.11 | 23.21 | 25.52 | 14.38 | 20.90 |

Table 4: Scores by Branch, Months Deployed, and Gender

*Leader Developmental Readiness*

Leader developmental readiness is a combination of one's motivation and ability to personally grow and develop. Leaders with higher levels of developmental readiness will be better able to reflect upon and make meaning out of events, challenges, and/or opportunities that can stimulate and accelerate positive leader development. Table 5 presents the mean scores for the respondents' motivation to develop. This is comprised of three components: intrinsic interests/goals (desire to grow and develop specifically as a leader); learning goal orientation (incremental mindset and learning-focused growth); and developmental efficacy (perceived ability to learn, grow, and develop). The range of scores is from 1 to 7 with a higher score indicating a greater perceived level of motivation. From the results, the respondents indicate that overall they are more intrinsically motivated to develop as a leader when compared to any other component. In contrast, they are less confident that they can develop and successfully employ the knowledge, skills, and abilities in certain leadership contexts.

| | INTRINSIC INTEREST/GOALS | LEARNING GOAL ORIENTATION | DEVELOPMENTAL EFFICACY |
|---|---|---|---|
| **Overall Mean Scores** | 6.17 | 5.91 | 5.28 |

Table 5: Motivation to Develop

Table 6 presents the mean scores for the respondents' ability to develop. This consists of three components: self awareness (identity clarity and stability and emotional awareness); complexity (integration and differentiation as well as social and self complexity); and meta-cognitive ability (knowledge of cognition and regulation of cognition). The range of scores is from 1 to 7 with a higher score indicating a greater perceived level of ability. The results show that respondents view their ability to develop in each of the components generally the same. In the extremes, they see their ability to differentiate as well as integrate various sources of information as greatest, and their ability to think beyond reflection and engage in deeper examination of their experiences as lowest.

| | SELF AWARENESS | COMPLEXITY | META-COGNITVE ABILITY |
|---|---|---|---|
| **Overall Mean Scores** | 5.32 | 5.37 | 5.26 |

Table 6: Ability to Develop

*Adaptability*

Adaptability was measured across seven dimensions. Table 7 presents the overall mean scores for each of these dimensions. The range of scores is from 1 to 5.

| | **Overall Mean Scores** |
|---|---|
| 1. **SOLVING PROBLEMS CREATIVELY** | 4.15 |
| 2. **DEALING WITH UNCERTAIN OR UNPREDICTABLE WORK SITUATIONS** | 3.87 |
| 3. **LEARNING NEW TASKS, TECHNOLOGIES, AND PROCEDURES** | 3.98 |
| 4. **DEMONSTRATING INTERPERSONAL ADAPTABILITY** | 4.09 |
| 5. **DEMONSTRATING CULTURAL ADAPTABILITY** | 4.21 |
| 6. **DEMONSTRATING PHYSICALLY ORIENTED ADAPTABILITY** | 4.11 |
| 7. **HANDLING WORK STRESS** | 3.60 |
| 8. **HANDLING EMERGENCIES OR CRISIS SITUATIONS** | 3.46 |

Table 7: Adaptability Dimensions

The score indicates the respondents' self assessment of effectiveness within each dimension. The higher score represents a greater perceived level of

22

effectiveness. The results show that the respondents believe they are less effective in handling emergency or crisis situations and most effective in demonstrating cultural adaptability. In general, however, the scores demonstrate a high level of adaptability.

*Organizational Culture and Leader Development*

As part of the on-going Army Profession Campaign, the Center for the Army Profession and Ethic (CAPE) conducted a series of surveys and focus group interviews on a wide range of topics relevant to the campaign. One open ended question is particularly relevant to the current discussion in this paper, namely: What do you recommend Senior Army Leaders do to improve unit/organization culture and climate?[52] The 251 COL/O6 responses to this question were analyzed, looking specifically for those comments that address (1) whether or not Army culture is supportive of learning agility and (2) leader development in general. Table 8 summarizes the responses with common themes.[53]

Considering the responses related to learning agility, the respondents recognize the importance in creating an environment that facilitates learning. Candor, initiative, empowerment, sense of self, creative problem solving, and encouraging differences of opinion are all factors that allow for learning agility to flourish. In a culture characterized by such characteristics, leaders will be more likely to seek, perform, and reflect, and less likely to be defensive and risk averse.

For those responses relevant to leader development, several are assignment related and speak to the idea of increasing broadening experiences. The respondents indicate the need to increase the diversity of assignments, to include assignments outside of the Army and in either the business or academic realm.

23

| Learning Agility Related (is the culture supportive?) | Leader Development Related |
|---|---|
| "…encourage initiative and creative problem solving." | "Senior Army Leaders owe their subordinate leaders, commissioned and enlisted, at all levels, the structured education and practical experiences that create the diverse set of tools necessary to succeed in VUCA environments." |
| "Accept candor and support difference of opinion…" | "What may be a better approach is to look where great commanders are assigned post command. Send them to the school house where they can continue to inspire the greatest number of junior officers and reinforce the character of the profession as well as what good leadership looks like." |
| "Allow for diverse opinions and points of view…" | "Incorporate the 360 degree leader feedback into Army selection and promotion boards." |
| "Continue to empower commanders and senior enlisted leaders to influence, build, develop, and lead their Soldiers and units." | "Poor military preparation of leaders: Most leaders fail to understand what it is to mentor, the committed time required. Army MUST train its force to understand the value of soft power; huge investment on the front end, lasting results at the tail." |
| "Empowering junior leaders, with proper oversight-leadership, will go a long way to improving the culture and climate of units across the Army." | "Require leaders to attend proven leadership courses that involve a self-assessment and group exercises to make them really think about leadership and to improve the way they communicate, provide recognition and feedback, and influence others." |
| "Encourage candor. If leaders don't know what people really think, they won't be able to know how their decisions are affecting others. There is no room for leaders who just want "yes men." | "Spend a week or short period of time at a university (Dean level) department to see just how broad their group of people are and how they work together. The diversity and inter-workings at a school is very unique and gives a very good perspective (appreciation). Maybe before BDE command." |
| "It takes someone with a strong sense of self to seek out opinions and perspectives contrary to those they hold." | |

Table 8: Army Culture Focus Group Responses

There is also an expressed desire to keep quality officers in the institutional Army teaching leadership and other relevant subjects to the next generation of officers. Often these officers are assigned to "non-schoolhouse" positions. Finally, there was a trend to include more multi-rater feedback in the Army development and evaluation process.

Discussion

The Army senior leaders who participated in this research are generally representative of the larger population. This allows several inferences with respect to the findings. First, one can infer that Army senior leaders have a perceived high level of leader developmental readiness. They view both their motivation to develop and ability to develop as high (although perceived motivation is higher). Next, senior leaders perceive themselves as adaptable, especially when it pertains to cultural adaptability and solving problems creatively.

Finally, for learning agility, Army senior leaders perceive themselves to be high on those behaviors that enhance learning agility – seeking, performing, and reflecting – but also high on those behaviors that potentially de-rail learning agility – risk aversion and defensiveness. Given that learning agility is the ability to apply previous learning and/or embrace learning in new, novel, or ill-defined environments, the conditions within the Army's culture may not currently exist to get the most out of this ability. To do this, leaders need to maximize the enhancing behaviors and minimize the de-railing behaviors. The responses to the open ended questions about Army culture show the need to create the conditions for learning and development, but point to the Army not being there yet. That the Army is "zero defect" was a common response when asked

25

what to fix in Army culture.  This creates an environment for risk aversion and defensiveness.

The proposed leader development model begins with leader developmental readiness.  High leader developmental readiness promotes learning agility in leaders, which results in adaptable leaders.  Army culture moderates these linkages, however, and determines to some degree whether development succeeds or fails.  This model requires further research in order to truly understand the value of its efficacy.  Time and measures of assessment other than self reporting will provide a more meaningful understanding of the model and will help to clarify direction of causality.  The current research suggests, however, that senior leaders have high developmental readiness, they are learning agile – to a point – and they are adaptable.  In the eyes of the population assessed in this study, Army culture is currently moderating learning agility in a negative manner by creating the conditions for defensiveness and risk aversion.

The current Army Leader Development Strategy (ALDS) states that the operational environment "demands that [the Army] develop leaders who ***understand*** the context of the factors influencing the military situation, ***act*** within that understanding, continually ***assess and adapt*** those actions based on the interactions and circumstances of the enemy and environment, ***consolidate*** tactical and operational opportunities into strategic aims, and be able to effectively ***transition*** from one form of operations to another."[54]  The model proposed in this research fits within this strategy, especially as it applies to learning agility.  Leaders who are able to apply previous learning and/or embrace new learning are exactly the leaders the Army Leader Development Strategy seeks to develop.

The ALDS is anchored in three paradigm shifts.[55]  The first is the effect of increased complexity and time.  Institutional policies and processes optimized for a world of mass and rapid decisive campaigns against predictable peer competitors must adapt to the new norm of uncertainty and protracted conflict.  The evidence is only beginning to be amassed, but early results look as though learning agile leaders are able to manage themselves in these challenging situations and deal with these new situations in a way that maximizes their performance and that of their subordinates.  The effect of decentralization requires the hierarchical Army to match tactical agility with institutional agility and to develop leaders who can create an environment of collaboration and trust to promote adaptation and innovation.  This can only happen if there is a culture that minimizes defensiveness and risk aversion, thereby allowing learning agile leaders to seek out new ways of doing things and reflecting on these new experiences to surface critical information.  Likewise, with the need to frame ill-structured problems, learning agile leaders can seek and reflect within a supportive culture in order to understand a problem and appreciate its complexities before seeking to solve it.

Limitations and Recommendations for Future Research

There are several limitations with this research.  Future research needs to account for these limitations.  First, the sample should be more representative of the larger population to allow for precision in generalizing the findings.  Also, all scores on the survey are self reported.  The incorporation of a multi-rater feedback system (peers, subordinates, supervisors) would provide for a more complete assessment of the survey measures.  In addition, a longitudinal study potentially would allow the researcher to

27

assess how and why learning agility, developmental readiness, and adaptability develop over time. Finally, the theoretical model outlines several links between the variables. These propositions are based on the existing research and literature on leader developmental readiness, learning agility, and adaptability. Future research should empirically test these relationships.

Table 9 shows the correlations between learning agility and several variables: leader developmental readiness (motivation to develop and ability to develop); adaptability; number of months deployed since September 11, 2001; number of months with current unit; and number of people supervised. Future research should focus on the significant correlations to further understand how and why these relationships exist and the direction of causality.

| | Motivation to Develop | Ability to Develop | Adaptability | Months Deployed Since 9/11 | Months in Unit | Number of People Supervised |
|---|---|---|---|---|---|---|
| Seeking | .377** | .468** | .467** | -0.077 | .042 | -.077 |
| Performing | .505** | .637** | .670** | -.035 | -.038 | .063 |
| Reflecting | .353** | .497** | .409** | .045 | .111 | -.087 |
| Defensiveness | -0.16 | -.129 | -.043 | -.026 | -.261* | .136 |
| Risk Aversion | .261* | .266* | .336** | -.031 | -.155 | -.097 |

** Correlation is significant at the 0.01 level (2-tailed)
* Correlation is significant at the 0.05 level (2-tailed)

Table 9: Correlations

Table 10 outlines the correlations between the overall learning agility construct and the specific variables in the theoretical model. Again, further research should explore these relationships in more detail.

| | Motivation to Develop | Ability to Develop | Adaptability |
|---|---|---|---|
| Learning Agility | .675** | .659** | .576** |

** Correlation is significant at the 0.01 level (2-tailed)
* Correlation is significant at the 0.05 level (2-tailed)

Table 10: Theoretical Model Correlations

## Conclusion

The purpose of this research is to elicit thought and discussion about current Army leader development systems and the qualities required of Army leaders. The current Army Profession campaign makes the case for a re-evaluation and assessment of the Army as a profession and the attributes of the Army Professional. Leadership entails the repetitive exercise of discretionary judgments, all highly moral in nature, and represents the core function of the professional's military art. Discretionary judgments are the coin of the realm in all professions; foremost in the military.[56] Leader development is an investment required to maintain the Army as a profession. The profession is maintained by leaders who place high priority on and invest themselves and the resources of the profession to develop professionals and future leaders at all levels.[57]

The mission of Army leader development is to educate, train, and provide experiences to progressively develop leaders to prevail in Full Spectrum Operations in a 21st Century security environment and to lead the Army Enterprise.[58] This requires a balanced commitment to the three pillars of leader development: training, education, and experience. As part of this process, Army systems must provide leaders with the motivation and the ability to develop, with the focus on developing learning agile leaders. These are the agile, adaptable, and innovative leaders that the Army requires. An uncertain and complex future security environment demands that Army leader development prepares leaders to operate with competence and confidence in ambiguous, frequently changing circumstances.[59] These are learning agile leaders.

## Endnotes

[1] Lopez, C. Todd. 2011. "Soldiers Top Priority for new CSA". *Army News Service*, 9 September.

[2] Bacon, Lance. 2011. "A Tested Top Warrior." *Army Times*, 19 September.

[3] Department of the Army. 2008. *Field Manual 3-0: Operations*. Washington, D.C.

[4] Ibid.

[5] Haskins, Casey. 2010. *A Good Answer to an Obsolete Question: The Army's Culture and Why It Needs to Change.*

[6] Ibid.

[7] Ibid.

[8] Vandergriff, Donald E. 2011. *One Step Forward, Two Steps Back: Mission Command versus the Army Personnel System*. The Institute of Land Warfare: Association of the United States Army.

[9] Ibid.

[10] Robertson, Chris and Sophie Gainey. 2009. "Getting off the Treadmill of Time". *Military Review*. November – December 2009.

[11] Snider, Don M. 2005. "The U.S. Army as a Profession." In *The Future of the Army Profession, 2$^{nd}$ Edition*, edited by Lloyd J. Matthews. Boston: McGraw-Hill.

[12] Ibid.

[13] Ibid.

[14] Burk, James. 2005. "Expertise, Jurisdiction, and Legitimacy of the Military Profession." In *The Future of the Army Profession, 2$^{nd}$ Edition*, edited by Lloyd J. Matthews. Boston: McGraw-Hill.

[15] Ibid.

[16] Snider. 2005.

[17] Department of the Army. 2010. *An Army White Paper: The Profession of Arms*. Combined Arms Center, TRADOC.

[18] Ibid. 1.

[19] This was previously presented in Snider, Don M. and Gayle L. Watkins. 2002. "Introduction." In *The Future of the Army Profession*, edited by Lloyd J. Matthews. Boston: McGraw-Hill.

[20] Department of the Army. 2010. 5.

[21] Pfaff, Tony. 2005. "Military Ethics in Complex Contingencies." In *The Future of the Army Profession, 2$^{nd}$ Edition*, edited by Lloyd J. Matthews. Boston: McGraw-Hill.

[22] Ibid. 410.

[23] Hannah, Sean T., John T. Eggers, and Peter L. Jennings. 2008. "Complex Adaptive Leadership: Defining What Constitutes Effective Leadership for Complex Organizational Contexts." In *Knowledge-Driven Corporation – Complex Creative Destruction*. 80-81.

[24] Ibid.

[25] Ibid. 102.

[26] Northouse, Peter G. 2010. *Leadership: Theory and Practice 5th Edition*. Los Angeles: SAGE Publications, Inc.

[27] Ibid. 3.

[28] Hannah et al. 2008. 103.

[29] Lacquement, Richard. 2005. "Mapping Army Professional Expertise and Clarifying Jurisdictions of Practice." In *The Future of the Army Profession, 2nd Edition*, edited by Lloyd J. Matthews. Boston: McGraw-Hill.

[30] Ibid. 225.

[31] Burke, Warner W. and Workgroup (Nathan Gerard, Adam Mitchinson, Robert Morris, and Kate Roloff). 2010. *Learning Agility Assessment*. Unpublished presentation.

[32] This has not been empirically tested. I offer this proposition based on my reading and analysis of the existing literature on adaptability and learning agility, and this will be the basis for future research.

[33] Hannah et al. 2008.

[34] Avolio, Bruce J. and Sean T. Hannah. 2008. "Developmental Readiness: Accelerating Leader Development." *Consulting Psychology Journal: Practice and Research* 60(4): 331-347.

[35] Burke et al. 2010.

[36] Schein, Edgar H. 1985. *Organizational Culture and Leadership*. San Francisco, CA: Jossey-Bass Publishers. 6-7.

[37] Hannah, Sean T. and Bruce J. Avolio. 2010. "Ready or Not: How do we Accelerate the Developmental Readiness of Leaders." *Journal of Organizational Behavior* 31: 1181-1187. 1182.

[38] Avolio and Hannah. 2008.

[39] This link between developmental readiness and learning agility is not empirically tested. However, I believe it is a reasonable proposition given the behaviors associated with learning agility and the outcomes of increased leader developmental readiness. This is an area for further research.

[40] Hannah and Avolio. 2010.

[41] Ibid.

[42] Ibid.

[43] Avolio and Hannah. 2008.

[44] This measure requires the express permission of Sean Hannah (sean.hannah@usma.edu).

[45] Pulakos, Elaine D. et al. 2002. "Predicting Adaptive Performance: Further Tests of a Model of Adaptability." *Human Performance* 15(4): 299-323.

[46] The Army data are from the Officer Master File, Office of Economic Manpower Analysis (West Point, NY).

The sample includes the current stock of active duty Army LTC and COL as of 30 September 2011. Branch Grouping: Other includes Judge Advocate General Corps, Chaplain Corps, Medical Corps, Medical Service Corps, Medical Specialist Corps, and Veterinary Corps. Most recent civilian graduate degree type reports the share of officers with at least one civilian graduate degree by type. Most recent civilian graduate degree type indicators are conditional upon having at least one civilian graduate degree. (e.g. Among O6's with at least 1 civilian graduate degree, 45.7 percent have a professional graduate degree.) Professional degree includes both Masters and Doctoral Degrees in professional fields (i.e. health, law, education). Masters includes the remaining non-professional or academic masters level degrees. Doctor includes the remaining non-professional or academic doctor level degrees.

[47] Pew Research Center. 2011. *The Military-Civilian Gap: War and Sacrifice in the Post-9/11 Era.* 5 Oct.

[48] The first percentage is for the Colonel population. The second percentage represents the gender breakdown for the US military.

[49] The DA Civilian respondents were the ones who reported no graduate degree. All of the officers in the sample reported having a graduate degree.

[50] Kolb, David A. 2007. *Kolb Learning Style Inventory.* Hay Group.

[51] Thoughts in this paragraph were gathered from discussions with Dr. Lee Knefelkamp, Professor, Teacher's College, Columbia University.

[52] From the Army Profession survey conducted by the Center for the Army Profession and Ethic. Contact CAPE for more details on survey (http://cape.army.mil/index.html).

[53] This is a summary of the responses and is not all inclusive. Many responses to this question were not relevant to learning agility or leadership. For those responses that were relevant to these topics, not all are included here. Many said the same thing, or something similar. I highlighted the common themes.

[54] TRADOC. "A Leader Development Strategy for a 21st Century Army." 25 November 2009.

[55] Ibid.

[56] Department of the Army. 2010.

[57] Ibid. 5.

[58] TRADOC. "A Leader Development Strategy for a 21st Century Army." 25 November 2009.

[59] Ibid.